For Ezra, Eden, and Noah

First edition published by Holders Hill Publishing in 2022

Copyright © Nathan Holder, 2022

The right of Nathan Holder to be identified as the Author of the Work has been asserted by him in accordance with the Copyright, Designs and Patents Act 1988

All rights reserved. No part of this publication may be reproduced, distributed, or transmitted in any form or by any means, including photocopying, recording, or other electronic or mechanical methods, without the prior written permission of the publisher, except in the case of brief quotations embodied in critical reviews and certain other noncommercial uses permitted by copyright law.

A Cataloguing-in-Publication catalogue record for this book is available from the British Library

ISBN - 978-1-7395839-0-3

www.thewhybooks.co.uk

Book layout and illustration by Charity Russell
www.charityrussell.com

# Where Are All The Instruments?
## West Africa

### Nathan Holder
#### Illustrated by Charity Russell

The group's next stop was Guinea-Bissau. They stood in front of a monument outside of the former Presidential Palace.

'This akonting reminds me of a guitar,' said Phoebe.

'It can have three, four or five strings!'

'Let's go back to class and show everyone what we found!' said Phoebe excitedly.

'Yes!' agreed Olivia. 'We can show everyone how to play these instruments and tell them about the places we saw!'

The Why Squad boarded their final plane and headed back to school.

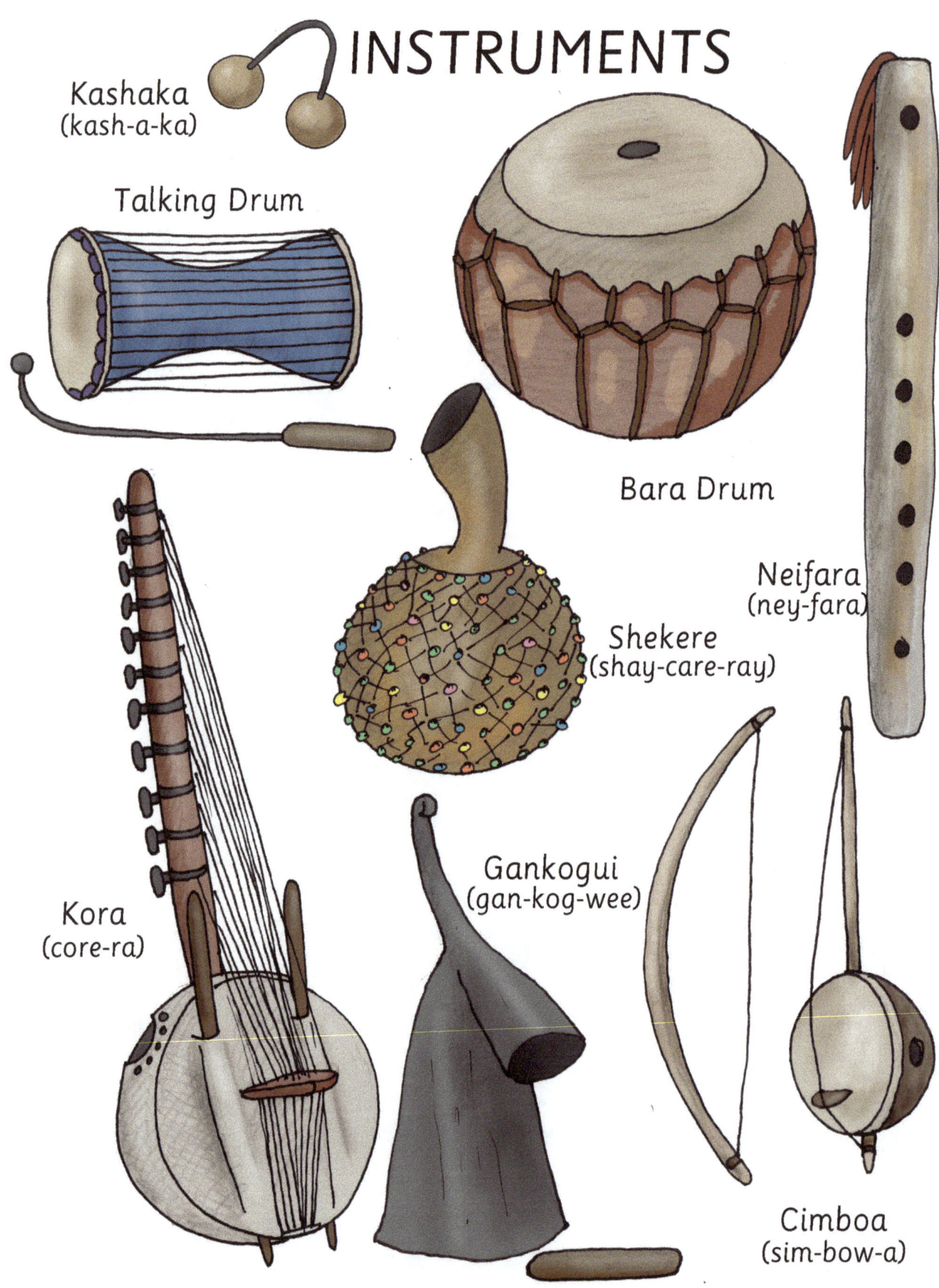

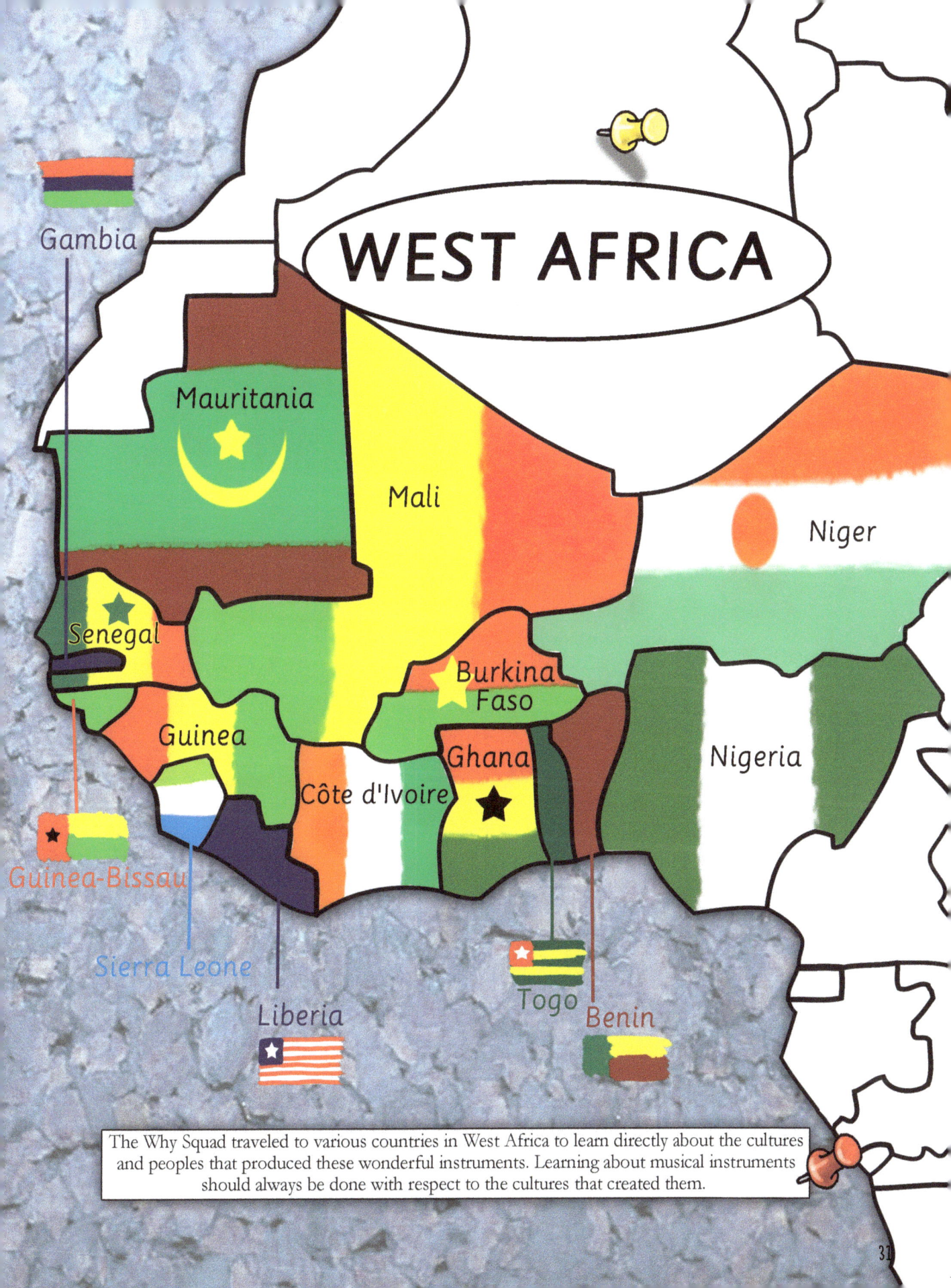

# Questions And Answers

Can you find all of the hidden instruments?

Can you find the hidden alien?

What is your favourite West African instrument?

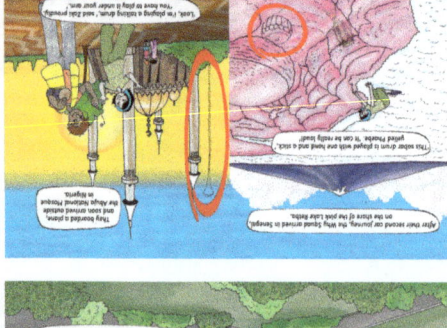

www.ingramcontent.com/pod-product-compliance
Lightning Source LLC
Chambersburg PA
CBHW051322110526
44590CB00031B/4440